Decision making is a huge part of the daily functional life of any individual, thus learning how to effectively make decisions are worth exploring. Though the experience of making decisions can be somewhat paralyzing at times it can also be fairly easy once the art is learned and practiced regularly. This book will get you on your way.

Alek Martinovic is an author and entrepreneur based in Serbia. Currently studying psychology, Alek is a travel junkie and an adventurous person. Hard-working and always willing to improve, he has a bright future ahead of him.

Decide to Decide

Alek Martinovic

Terms and Conditions

LEGAL NOTICE

Table Of Contents

Foreword

Decision making is a huge part of the daily functional life of any individual, thus learning how to effective make decisions are worth exploring. Though the experience of making decisions can be somewhat paralyzing at times it can also be fairly easy once the art is learnt and practiced regularly. This book will get you on your way.

Decide To Decide
Guide To Arriving At A Decision

Chapter 1:

Making A Decision Basics

Synopsis

Perhaps some elements to explore first, should be the things to avoid or identify as negative when trying to effectively make a decision. Wanting too much certainly or a high level of positive elements to be apparent before acting on the decision making will eventually cause the individual to stall and even avoid the decision process altogether.

The Basics

Perfectionist types often fall into this category and this causes serious problems especially with regard to making business decisions. Making decision under emotional or whimsical mindset is also something to be avoided as the thought process at this point is often unclear and prejudicial.

Another folly is the need to have lots of edification before making the decision. Some people are simply reluctant to decide on anything without the consensus of the masses.

Most wise people learn from their mistakes and exercise better judgments when making decision the next time round and this is a very valuable lesson to learn instead of continuously making the same mistakes.

Making a conscious effort to make a decisive decision before moving on to the next endeavor would be a good habit to build upon. Refusing to overly focus on every small detail does eventually help in the process of making a decision promptly and effectively.

Avoid second guessing every thought and action that may result from the decision made. Accept the possible degree of things not going as planned and make the decision to move on anyway. Sometimes effective decision making requires the individual to take certain levels of risks, therefore being overly cautious and sensible can be stumbling block.

Chapter 2:

Nail Down The Problem

Synopsis

Understanding the problem first is perhaps the most effective way of ensuring a suitable solution is found or at the very least the problem is rationally considered. The process of collecting as much information as possible to assist in the process of identifying the problem should be the first course of action. Jumping to conclusions without the relevant information to back such assumptions will only lead to more problems and complications.

What's The Issue

Several techniques can be used in the quest to nail down the problem, some of which may include direct observation of the situation at hand, a consensus of the styles being currently used, brainstorming, data analysis and many more.

Using previous case studies as a possible link to solving the problem is also another way to finding solutions. Analyzing the problem and being ready to consider the range of solutions available should help lessen if not completely solve it.

Having adequate resources available in terms of budget, expertise, information and other helpful elements does help lessen the pressure considerably, thus giving all concerned the leeway to better achieve a solution.

Some find that describing the problem in detail gives better understanding to the overall picture of the true situation at hand. With this clearer picture of the problem evident, the solution can be better tailored to suit the problem solving exercise.

In other cases it was found that having a clearly specified list of problems that could possibly be linked or cross referenced to the problem at hand proved to be very useful indeed.

When starting out on any endeavor it would be somewhat of an advantage to also take some time to note possible problems that might arise through the course of the set up exercise and have the necessary solutions at hand to ensure there are no serious repercussions.

Chapter 3:

Identify And Evaluate Alternatives

Synopsis

Selecting solutions without proper identification and evaluation of the problem at hand can be costly and eventually contribute to an even bigger mess, thus there is a need to carefully consider each aspect of the problem individually and collectively before any firm action is taken.

Figure It Out

When in search of the best and most desirable solution not to mention a cost effective one, as analysis of the opposing factors and complimenting factors should be taken into consideration.

Ideally multi-purpose programs and exercises should be presented before any firm action is taken as the more alternative presented the more viable options become available to ensure the best course of action is chosen.

A comfortable and balanced solution can be easier to find if all alternatives are simultaneously viewed and their individual impacts are monitored.

Basically the evaluation process should not function as a justifying tool but more as a refinement tool to any alternative option chosen.

Ideally several opposing and complimenting disciplines should work together to compare and investigate thoroughly any alternatives presented through the various analytical techniques already in place.

However being open to explore other techniques which have yet to be tried should also be considered, however this should only become a viable option if the necessary supporting data on all possible outcomes are fairly clearly outlined.

Also to be noted at this point, is that all analysis done are definitely going to be subjected to variables depending on the main aim of the decision making process.

Most evaluations are done based on the driving factor behind the decision that needs to be made. These decisions may include the need to improve on a service or product or to simply correct an existing problem which is causing loss of revenue or production time.

Knowing all the alternatives available makes the decision making more effective and workable.

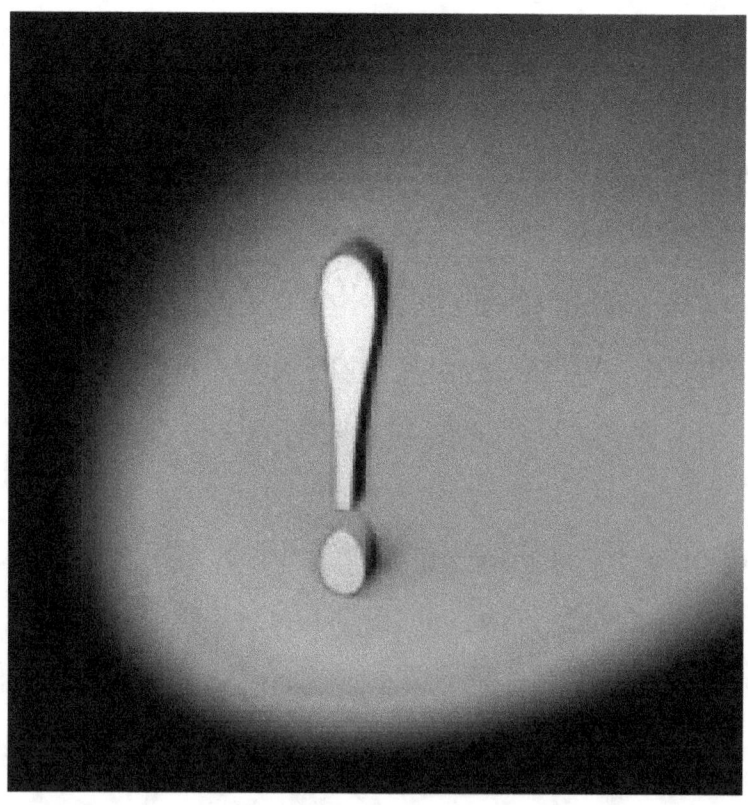

Chapter 4:

Gather Data On Your Selections

Synopsis

Whenever a selection is done on anything, the relevant data is normally collected and analyzed before any decision is made. The data collection ideally should be extensive and comprehensive to encompass any possible outcome scenarios.

All The Info

Several points of interest should be considered such as the identification of potential barriers to the evaluation process. A system should ideally be in place to handle any potential barriers related to the project being evaluated.

Then the exercise of addressing these potential barriers should be handled with some level of proficiency to ensure a workable outcome. An overview should also be provided for the different and possibly varying data collected through the course of exploring the evaluation process.

Based on the data collected it would also be advantageous to have a checklist or a list of probable questions that may be put forth during a discussion session through the course of the evaluation process.

These anticipated questions will also help keep the focus on identifying the probable and most suitable solutions possible.

Other beneficial elements to be included in the data gathering exercise should be a workable framework for the organizing, analyzing and interpreting of the data to be presented in a report format based on the results found.

If a more complex data gathering is required then the overview of both quantitative and qualitative data should be formatted and highlighted during the presentation process for all concerned to mull over.

Incorporating the practice of identifying the various audiences within the project and the types of streamlined information from the data they should be privy too is also beneficial in terms of time and understanding of the data presented.

Open discussions should be held to address the data selection available, as this would also help to further explore the evaluation aspect of the exercise.

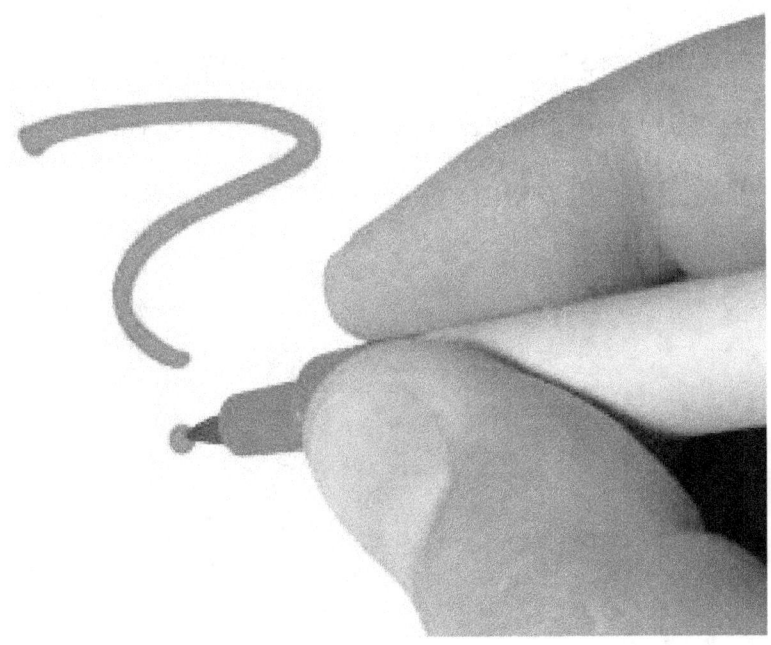

Chapter 5:

Use Common Sense And How You Feel

Synopsis

Most individual who are considering venturing into any sort of endeavor would start gathering and reading material linked to their particular choice in mind.

Trying to emulate or even copy some of the proven methods is probably a very common notion that most would follow.

However with this also come the very important realization that at some point the individual common sense and feeling or gut feelings as some would call it should take precedence over what has been learnt from books and seminars and the likes.

Use Your Brain

For most successful entrepreneurs this common sense and gut feeling is what they attest to being the main guiding beacon when it came to making decisions, major or minor.

However this in no way negates the fact that all relevant information should be gathered and understood before the said decision is reached, but both the elements of common sense and feelings do play a somewhat crucial role within the decision making process.

When decision are made with these two elements being taken into consideration, the general feeling of being comfortable is always a plus point as this is what will drive the individual to continue to strive for excellence.

Relying on good contacts, processes, strategies, margins, team work, among others does have its merits but at the same time the other two very personal elements of common sense and feelings should not be ignored altogether.

The fore mentioned requirements are all very necessary for any endeavor considered and coupling it with the other two personalized element should create the beginnings of a successful and workable scenario.

A lot of times simply based on the information learnt or experienced from the past does allow the individual some level on insight into the matter at hand which is not necessarily evident from the data presented at that point in time. Therefore completely ignoring the common sense or feelings aspect of the equation may prove to be a folly indeed.

Chapter 6:

Implement Your Decision

Synopsis

The exercise of implementing a decision made can be a very complicated or very easy process, as it all depends on the individual and how committed he or she is to the decision itself.

Pit It Into Affect

The first and probably the most important barrier to overcome is within the individual itself and how high a level of conviction is of the decision about to be implemented.

If the conviction element based on the choice of the decision is strong and certain, then the implementation element of the exercise becomes a lot easier and smoother.

The implementation of the decision should encompass the completing or performing of the decision making process which would in turn give rise to the actually course of action to be taken based on the said decision being made.

The results achieved from the implementation process should also be given due consideration as rational decision making if often based on a lot of underlying elements.

These underlying elements that could affect the implementing process may surface in the form of the current state of mind, the physical condition of the decision maker, the volatile business scenarios and many other coinciding factors.

During the implementing phase of the decision making process, most individual tend to question the viability of the decision made.

Questions like whether the decision chosen is the best for that particular situation or whether the decision is even the correct course of action and many other similar misgiving are often likely to surface.

Wrapping Up

Having the confidence in the choice made is always very important as it directly impacts the implementation process.

Decisions that result in freedom to have personal control should be the ones to align one's self with, as it is with the implementation of these kinds of decisions that allows the endeavors to grow both financially and physically to greater heights always.